IT'S TIME TO EAT DILL

It's Time to Eat DILL

Walter the Educator

Silent King Books
A WhichHead Entertainment Imprint

Copyright © 2025 by Walter the Educator

All rights reserved. No part of this book may be reproduced in any manner whatsoever without written per- mission except in the case of brief quotations embodied in critical articles and reviews.

First Printing, 2024

Disclaimer

This book is a literary work; the story is not about specific persons, locations, situations, and/or circumstances unless mentioned in a historical context. Any resemblance to real persons, locations, situations, and/or circumstances is coincidental. This book is for entertainment and informational purposes only. The author and publisher offer this information without warranties expressed or implied. No matter the grounds, neither the author nor the publisher will be accountable for any losses, injuries, or other damages caused by the reader's use of this book. The use of this book acknowledges an understanding and acceptance of this disclaimer.

It's Time to Eat DILL is a collectible early learning book by Walter the Educator suitable for all ages belonging to Walter the Educator's Time to Eat Book Series. Collect more books at WaltertheEducator.com

USE THE EXTRA SPACE TO TAKE NOTES AND DOCUMENT YOUR MEMORIES

DILL

It's time to eat, let's take a look,

It's Time to Eat

Dill

A leafy herb for every cook!

With frilly fronds so soft and light,

Green and feathery, what a sight!

Dill grows tall and sways so free,

Waving gently just like a tree.

Its scent is fresh, so strong and bright,

A little sniff, oh, what delight!

We pick some dill and hold it tight,

Its tiny leaves are such a sight!

A little tickle on my nose,

A lovely smell the garden grows!

Now wash it well and shake it dry,

Watch the water splash and fly!

A little rinse, then chop, chop, chop,

Into a bowl, plip, plop, plop!

It's Time to Eat

Dill

Sprinkle dill on fish or rice,

Add a little, oh, so nice!

In a salad, soup, or dip,

It makes the taste just zing and zip!

Dill in pickles? Yes, it's true!

That's what gives them flavor too!

Crunchy, tangy, oh so fun,

A tasty snack for everyone!

It's good for you, it helps you grow,

Gives you strength from head to toe!

So many ways to eat this treat,

Dill is fresh and fun to eat!

Mix it in a butter spread,

Put some on a piece of bread!

In a sandwich, big or small,

It's Time to Eat

Dill

Dill makes flavors best of all!

So when you see these leaves so bright,

Pick some dill, it's just right!

Try a taste, don't be shy,

A little herb to make food fly!

Now we're full and feeling fine,

Dill has helped at dinner time!

A tiny plant with flavor grand,

It's Time to Eat

Dill

A tasty treat from garden land!

ABOUT THE CREATOR

Walter the Educator is one of the pseudonyms for Walter Anderson. Formally educated in Chemistry, Business, and Education, he is an educator, an author, a diverse entrepreneur, and he is the son of a disabled war veteran. "Walter the Educator" shares his time between educating and creating. He holds interests and owns several creative projects that entertain, enlighten, enhance, and educate, hoping to inspire and motivate you. Follow, find new works, and stay up to date with Walter the Educator™

at WaltertheEducator.com

www.ingramcontent.com/pod-product-compliance
Lightning Source LLC
LaVergne TN
LVHW052012060526
838201LV00059B/3982